BLACK LIVES MATTER!
NO JUSTICE! NO PEACE!
SAY THEIR NAMES!

Koshin Hanson
1610 N Prospect Ave Apt 1003
Milwaukee, WI 53202

I AM A ROHINGYA

I AM A ROHINGYA
*Poetry from the Camps
& Beyond*

Edited & introduced by
James Byrne & Shehzar Doja

with a Preface by
John Kinsella

2019

Published by Arc Publications
Nanholme Mill, Shaw Wood Road
Todmorden, OL14 6DA, UK
www.arcpublications.co.uk

Copyright in the poems © individual poets as named, 2019
Copyright in the translation © individual translators as named, 2019
Copyright in the Introduction © James Byrne & Shehzar Doja, 2019
Copyright in the Preface © John Kinsella, 2019
Copyright in the present edition © Arc Publications Ltd, 2019

Design by Tony Ward

978 1911469 69 8 (pbk)

Cover photograph by Fojit Sheikh Babu,
by kind permission of the photographer

This book is in copyright. Subject to statutory exception and to provisions of relevant collective licensing agreements, no reproduction of any part of this book may take place without the written permission of Arc Publications Ltd.

**Arc International Poets
Series Editor: James Byrne**

*This book is dedicated to all Rohingya
displaced from their homes*

*To those who have died and
those who have survived
in the ongoing struggle
to achieve basic human rights*

and

*to those who continue to hope
for a better life.*

CONTENTS

Acknowledgements / 9
Preface / 11
Editors' Introduction:
A New Rohingya Poetics / 13
Riversongs of the Rohingyas / 18

MAYYU ALI / 23
That's Me, A Rohingya
ANONYMOUS / 26
Lovesong
RO MEHROOZ / 27
The Cut Bud
THIDA SHANIA / 28
First Day at School
YAR TIN / 29
About Those Born into This Place
PACIFIST FAROOQ / 32
My Life
ZAKI OVAIS / 33
Someone I'm Afraid Of
MAUNG HLA SHWE / 34
An Orphan
MAROON MOON / 35
Dad
RO PACIFIST / 36
Give Me a Chance to Restart This Life
ANONYMOUS / 38
Lament (a Fisherman's Song)
RO ANAMUL HASAN / 40
Being Rohingya
RO MEHROOZ / 42
Blot Out
RO B. M. HAIRU / 43
Behind Life
MAYYU ALI / 44
They're Kind Killers
THIDA SHANIA / 45
Save Me

MAUNG HLA SHWE / 46
My Arakan
AZAD MOHAMMED / 48
Misfortune
YASMIN ULLAH / 49
Birth
MAUNG ABDUL KHAN / 56
New Hope
MAROON MOON / 57
Our Fairytale
ZAKI OVAIS / 58
Water
RO B. M. HAIRU / 59
Tell Me What We are Guilty Of!
YAR TIN / 60
Too Much Bitterness
AHTARAM SHINE / 62
Memory of Torture
MAROON MOON / 63
How?
MAYYU ALI / 64
A Rohingya Refugee
PACIFIST FAROOQ / 65
The Heart's Burning Smell
RO MEHROOZ / 66
Broken Mirror
MAUNG ABDUL KHAN / 67
Survivor
YASMIN ULLAH / 68
The Unfamiliar Home
ANONYMOUS / 70
Mother Arakan
RO MEHROOZ / 71
Hasna Hena / Night-blooming Jasmine

Notes / 72

Afterword: An Interview with Mayyu Ali / 74

Contributors / 80

ACKNOWLEDGEMENTS

Thanks to the following people who have made this anthology of Rohingya poetry possible:, Mayyu Ali, Robert Anderson, Clare Pollard, Daniel Simon, Alam Khorshed at Bistaar, Tony Ward and Angela Jarman at Arc, Parveen & Sandeep Parmar, Tasleem Shakur, Jessica Tillings, all the staff at Friendship NGO, particularly Osman, Samsur, Shihab and especially Runa Khan for enabling our workshops in the camps. Thanks to Bilkis Akther and Kenneth Wong for helping with translation and transcription. Above all, we'd like to thank each one of the extraordinarily dedicated Rohingya poets and singers we have worked with.

Several of the poems included here – including earlier versions of some of the texts – were first published in *Modern Poetry in Translation*, *The Rohingya Art Garden* and *World Literature Today*. 'Lovesong' is published in *Poems from the Edge of Extinction: An Anthology of Poetry in Endangered Languages*, ed. Chris McCabe, (John Murray Press, 2019).

PREFACE

I Am a Rohingya implores the world to listen to the spirit of a people who have experienced, and continue to experience, some of the worst human rights abuses, but who, even under extreme duress and the constant reality of violence from the Myanmar state, know the spirit and intactness of their voice, their right to be a people and to live in the land that is their home. The suppression of the Rohingya by the machinery of British colonialism, then the military dictatorship, and the failure of post-dictatorship government to arrest the attack on the Rohingya and what is essentially an apartheid condition, have brought the people to speak out of their refugee camps along the border with Bangladesh, to find hope in language and the aurality of their language, to see their poetry on the page, and to make poetry do the work it needs to do so that outsiders can hear, can understand.

The remarkable Rohingya poet Mayyu Ali says in an interview with editor James Byrne that concludes this collection, a collection I consider a most important document of creative utterance: 'Writing for Rohingya people is activism. For me, a Rohingya, and a victim of the slow-burning genocide in Myanmar, imagism is far removed from activism.' And in this is the absolute truth of these poems – they must speak out, because they are from a crisis that must be addressed right now. Nonetheless, a powerful imagism of life-awareness, of what is being denied an entire people as well as every individual, speaks constantly and powerfully under every expression of the reality. The beauty of the land and forest that are being denied a people, the beauty of the people's cultural expression and their rights to their own history as well as a shared history, are denied, and these poems refuse this denial – these poems claim the beauty back.

This collection is a call to readers to listen and help, to bring hope. It's an affirmation of a strong community who know who they are. The energy and zest of language, of being able to speak at an angle from life itself, enhances their lives. I hope that it helps bring optimism and material improvement to the lives of the Rohingya, and that they can return safely to their home and be treated as a people with the rights of all other people. There is brilliance in here!

John Kinsella

INTRODUCTION

A NEW ROHINGYA POETICS
James Byrne

At the end of April 2019, Shehzar Doja and I travelled to Bangladesh to work with Rohingya refugees. Our aim was to set up the first ever creative writing workshops in the Cox's Bazaar camps where over one million people live in perilous conditions. Traumatised and stateless, they each have a story to tell about the horrific scenes they have experienced: the burning down of villages in Arakan, their home in Myanmar; genocide, rape and torture. *I Am a Rohingya* is a poetic response from those who have survived. It is a book that seeks both to celebrate and to document the powerful new voices of Rohingya poetry – voices that are direct, activist, and toughened by what they have had to suffer.

Cox's Bazaar is huge, the size of a small city, and stretches over more than twenty camps.[1] The area is named after Captain Hiram Cox who, working for the East India Company between 1797 and 1799, assigned 'waste lands' to thousands of 'emigrants and refugees' – when setting up the camps, Cox said he wanted to create a 'choky' (prison) for those arriving from Rakhine State.

For over two hundred years, the Rohingya have been forcibly moved out of their homes in Rakhine, and the present exodus, the result of violence in August 2017 on the part of the Burmese military (Tatmadaw) and Burmese Buddhist monks against the Rohingya, looks set to be prolonged, with no real or safe plans for repatriation. The camps are crowded and many can't even get in. Two hundred thousand Rohingya are currently stranded in a deadly no-man's land, or 'genocide zone', between Myanmar and Bangladesh, and are frequently killed or arrested by the Burmese army.[2]

---

[1] The camps are actually situated in the Teknaf and Ukhia Districts of Bangladesh, close to the town of Cox's, but most people refer to the area of the camps as Cox's Bazaar.

[2] Various reports of this have appeared in the media, emphasising the precariousness of Rohingya trying to flee Myanmar but with nowhere to go: https://www.trtworld.com/opinion/rohingya-trapped-inside-a-genocide-zone-26095

If you visit the camps today, you encounter – despite the presence of International Non-governmental Organisations (INGOs) – a people living in quarantine in a dust-dry, soil-eroded land, their huts dangerously balanced, airless in the boiling sun. It's remarkable to think these 'buildings' survived the latest monsoon. On the day I write this, a massive cyclone surges past India's East coast, heading towards Bangladesh. On our second day of workshops in the camps, a large fire broke out. As various governments kick the fate of the Rohingya people around courts and foreign offices, the Rohingya themselves experience the day-to-day difficulties of living in the camps, trying to look forward but haunted by the past. How can anybody keep living like this? The fact that we received such high-quality poetry from people who are experiencing hardships unimaginable to us in the West, is remarkable in itself, and is a testament to each poet's personal bravery, intelligence and dedication to their writing.

The two-day workshops in the camps mainly focused on metaphor, imagery and repetition. In the Friendship Learning Centre (a beautifully designed bamboo building standing out against the frail, tarpaulined huts in the distance), Shehzar and I discussed poems and poetics from T. S. Eliot to Mina Loy to Tomas Tranströmer, setting various exercises and workshopping the poems that the participants had begun to draft. We emphasised the possibilities of developing the senses, of inviting the reader into the poem as a participant to allow them to 'experience' the poem. As part of this, we discussed the importance in imagistic terms of showing as well as telling, taking care, when advocating such a creative approach, to be sensitive to those who had witnessed or experienced unspeakable atrocities. We considered the possibilities of breath and organic form and did exercises that involved the lyric, collage, ekphrasis. I remember re-entering the room after a break to see our twenty participants, pens in hand, huddled over Shehzar's phone as it blasted out instrumental music over the border camp traffic. Fifteen minutes into the first day of workshops, the call to prayer sounded over the camp speakers and I asked the poets to write something about the texture of the muezzin's voice, or the silences between his recitation of the Koran.

The participants were extraordinarily attentive, keen to develop and to try things out that were, in some cases, entirely new to them. As the young Rohingya poet Mayyu Ali discusses in the 'Afterword' at the end of this anthology, in Myanmar, if you were born Rohingya, you were lucky to receive any kind of extensive education, let alone be considered a poet, and several poems in this book explore the denial of a basic right to education. While many of the workshop participants had written poems before, others were writing their very first poems. There are, I believe, many exceptional poems in this anthology, although I don't intend to single out particular poets. One of the things that impressed me about the workshop group was its sense of community spirit, in itself a way the poets were able to survive. Indeed, the word 'Rohingya' appears in many of the poems here and various poets use the pen-name 'Ro' to emphasise the importance of identity to a people who have been ethnically cleansed and denied basic citizenship rights. Often the poets explore the fragility of identity, writing about Arakan or Cox's Bazaar as they live with the painful memories and losses of the past whilst confronting the uncertainty of the future. There are several poems that appeal directly to the reader for action, and there are poems of graphic violence, of blood(shed) and genocide (both words appear variously throughout the book). This is unsurprising when you speak to INGO schoolteachers in the camps who explain that children as young as four are drawing pictures of helicopters dropping bombs, of people being shot. These are the memories on which they were raised.

Although much of the work here is direct, other poems are less so; some deploy a different tone, are more linguistically or formally playful, some look forward with hope, strong in the (vital) belief that things can change. The folk songs (which Shehzar discusses below) are also different in tone, as you will hear if you listen to the original recordings made in the camps on YouTube ('Lovesong'[3] on p. 26 https://youtu.be/XNTs2GWcLAE and 'Mother Arakan' on p. 70 https://youtu.be/dyp9xDlBVpg). Most of the poets have decided to write in English, perhaps in an attempt to reach a larger audience and to appeal to the powers that be, but there are also two poems

---

[3] You can also see a video recording made in the camps of 'Lovesong', an anonymous folk song sung by Jam Alam, on https://drive.google.com/file/d/1zy2POVKJb8PtNR3xosUI6rIuZzszT67Q/view

which are translated from the Burmese, three songs transcribed from the Rohingya language and one poem translated from the Rohingya.[4] Rohingya is similar to Bengali-Assamese and is also related to the Chittagonian dialect spoken in Bangladesh. It is more than two hundred years old and written (if it is written at all) in a script very similar to Arabic, or by using the Roman alphabet.

Prior to visiting Bangladesh, and during my year-long correspondence with Mayyu Ali, I had made contact with a few Rohingya poets who had managed to get out of the camps. These poets are living in exile overseas or studying in Bangladesh under invented names, understandably worrying each day about whether their real identities might be discovered. Before we visited the camps in April, Mayyu and several other Rohingya poets joined us for an event in Chittagong which was preceded by a select but historic workshop comprising four male poets and one female poet.

Although we had tried to involve female poets, the workshop participants in the camps were all male; no women would attend the workshops if they involved men. Different as it is, this experience took me back to when I was researching *Bones Will Crow: 15 Contemporary Burmese Poets* (Arc, 2012). I remember how very difficult it was then to find poems written by women in Myanmar, and the same is true now of the Rohingya.[5] There is, however, some evidence that things are slowly changing, due in large part to education, health awareness and counselling programmes run by INGOs and NGOs. Perhaps there are also cultural and religious paradigms at work. That said, *I Am a Rohingya* does manage to include several significant

---

[4] 'About Those Born into This Place' (p. 29) and 'Too Much Bitterness' (p. 60) are translated from Burmese; the songs 'Lovesong' (p. 26), 'Lament' (p. 38) and 'Mother Arakan (p. 70) are transcribed from Rohingya; and Ro Mehrooz's 'Night-blooming Jasmine', the final poem in this anthology (which may also be considered a song) is translated from Rohingya. You can hear this poem read in the Rohingya language on https://soundcloud.com/user-951473637/ro-mehrooz-hasna-hena-night-blooming-jasmine.

[5] My sister-in-law, an expert in international global health who has visited the refugee camp in Cox's Bazaar several times to support existing health programmes for Rohingya, found evidence to suggest that Rohingya women are often living entirely domesticated lives, while others are unable to undergo basic medical procedures without male consent.

contributions by female poets; indeed, the longest poem in the book is by a woman. But there is a lot more work to be done in addressing gender inequalities in Rohingya society as our workshops revealed, and in my view, an edition of poems by female Rohingya poets would empower women more in the community and give them a more prominent voice.

Despite the current situation in Myanmar – its slide backwards on human rights, and the strong-arm tactics of the Tatmadaw, coupled with Aung San Su Kyi's deplorable silence on the treatment of the Rohingya – the picture is more complex than most can imagine, and some Burmese poets are, I am sure, sympathetic to the treatment of the Rohingya. One thing that international travel has taught me is that in every country there are many good people, persecuted and oppressed by their own governments. I know for a fact that there are activist poets in Myanmar who are simply too afraid to speak out, given previous genocidal operations. Most people in Myanmar will know someone who has been imprisoned, tortured or killed by the Burmese military under Generals / Dictators Than Shwe and Ne Win. This, to some degree, echoes the experiences of Rohingya survivors who will know someone who has suffered at the hands of the Tatmadaw – a moment of chilling symmetry perhaps. And yet the fact remains that it is the Rohingya who have suffered more than any ethnic minority in Myanmar for hundreds of years, even before the British arrived with their ideas of 'divide and rule'.

In the final hour of our workshop in the camps, Shehzar and I asked all the poets involved to send us a few poems, with the idea of publishing a a pamphlet of their work. The deadline was extremely tight, as we had only one week to edit anything that came through. Sometimes we received fifteen poems in a single day and we would edit the work and send it back to the poets for comment and approval, an extension of the workshop process itself. Very quickly we realised that *I Am a Rohingya* would be bigger than we first thought, book-length, focusing on a new Rohingya poetics and serving as the first anthology of Rohingya poetry to be published in the English language. Hopefully, further books will follow as the Rohingya community continues to channel its creativity in speaking out about the oppression and violence it has suffered over the centuries, and which it continues to endure.

We hope you are as inspired by these poems as we have been, and that in reading this selection, you feel impelled to bring about change. The Rohingya are, without doubt, one of the most persecuted people who live on our shared earth. And they are speaking to you now.

3 May 2019

RIVERSONGS OF THE ROHINGYAS
Shehzar Doja

Around August of 2017, news started arriving in Bangladesh of something terrible happening in Myanmar. Although the deltaic country had been host to numerous Rohingya refugees in the past, the influx this time was unrelenting. People could sense something was different. Day after day, the newspaper was reporting similar stories – it felt unreal. Bangladesh, having

been victim to numerous atrocities during the 1971 war for independence, was opening the door for the Rohingya refugees. Bangladesh, a tiny country with a population of so many million people, was saying 'What is one million more?', a sentiment shared publicly by the Prime Minister. This was a truly humane moment in the country's brief history.

I visited the refugee camps in September of 2017 for the first time and listened to first-hand accounts. It was only later, much later, that the world began to acknowledge the truth of what was happening in Myanmar – ethnic cleansing, genocide in a neighbouring country. During my initial visit, I began to notice how all the NGOs' and governmental bodies' focus was on healthcare and emergency relief, as it ought to be. But something vital was missing. Where were the archives of written literature, poetry and songs? The simple truth is that the ethnic Rohingya population, which has existed for several centuries, was being systemically purged of its identity including, essentially, its culture, in a manner reminiscent of great ethnic purges of the past.

There is a section of the Naf river that shares borders with Myanmar and Bangladesh. Where rivers come together,

COX'S BAZAAR – PHOTO: AZAD MOHAMMED

eventually to greet the Bay of Bengal, so do two cultures – in the form of a shared historical reverence for oral traditions and songs. Recording, transcribing, translating and sharing – these are important in order to help keep traditions alive, as is the nurturing of new talented poets amongst a community who have been systematically denied access to higher education for over forty years.

The songs were collected over different trips. It has been a great privilege to be able to listen to and record some of these, to have them transcribed by Bilkis Akhter, a Rohingya speaker, and eventually to translate them from a text that I was familiar with.

The three songs published within this book sung by Jani Alam are diverse in both tune and theme, yet a common thread seemed to emerge from a shared and sincere arc of yearning and reflection. These particular folk-songs (as far as I am aware) have been passed down, not rewritten but rather added to, layered as common practice, reflecting a more modern ambiance and construction of place. Songs in this tradition, sometimes spanning centuries, have an uncanny ability to transmute – from appearing uncomplicated on the surface to refracting deep and sincere truths from within an existing communal sensitivity. Bearing this in mind, and working alongside Jani Alam's thoughts in note form, I set about translating transcriptions of the songs into a modern poetic frame for further accessibility. Jani's sheer joy at glimpsing 'Lovesong' (p. 26) in *Modern Poetry in Translation* and hearing news of other forthcoming publications was a response that completely vindicated my approach. Although 'Lovesong' is a retelling of a tragic tale of love, it cleverly delves into universal motifs of fear and uncertainty –

I discover Hajera's fragrance on the bird's handkerchief.

with an almost seer-like prediction to complete its foreboding:

You catch yourself slipping and falling
on the narrow road,
a black water jug – cracked on a dark night.

The never-ending peril that looms for the Rohingya is another constant expressed in these folksongs.

That fisherman, he lures me – laughing, laughing

'That fisherman' is eerily reminiscent of an angler fish drawing in its prey, or is this a subtle political stance? The lost protagonist is wonderfully layered in subtext, leaving us listeners to ponder upon the precariousness of fate.

'Mother Arakan', a song divided into two narrative sections (of which our published version is one) is a staunch rallying call for the singer's countrymen, that peers with deep nostalgia and yearning into a lost motherland.

Oh these! – assortments and abundance of fruits, such richness we have discarded – on the path to these other shores

There is such dignity within these songs, of what was and was subsequently taken away; a penetrative thread that permeates many of the poems in this collection. Songs like these are such an important prism into exploring the rich but overlooked cultural heritage of the Rohingya. It is my sincerest hope that these folk-songs act as a catalyst for more research into this intriguing world and for its haunting tunes to find their path to a wider audience.

5 May 2019

MAYYU ALI

THAT'S ME, A ROHINGYA

When I was born,
I was not a baby like you are.
Without a birth certificate,
Just like death.

When I was one,
I was not a child like you are.
Without a nation,
Just like a pet.

When I was at school,
I wasn't a student like you are.
Without a Burmese face,
Just like the bleakness of the future.

When I was in another village,
I wasn't a resident like you are.
Seeking approval overnight,
Just like a crazed detainee.

When I pass through my town,
I'm not a citizen like you are.
Holding Form-4 authorisation,
Just like a nomad.

When I go to university,
I'm not a fresher like you are.
Denied professionalism, a major,
Just illegitimate.

When I approach people,
I'm not acceptable like you are.
Suffering apartheid and chauvinism,
Just like quarantine.

When I want to marry,
I'm not a fiancé like you are.
Approved for marriage,
Just like an alien.

When I want to repair my hut,
I'm not allowed to like you are.
Facing palpable denial,
Just like an invader.

When I arrange a little trade,
I'm not a vendor like you are.
Ongoing, restricted, confiscated,
Just like a pauper.

When I apply for the civil service,
I'm not a candidate like you are.
Receiving the motive of rejection,
Just like someone segregated.

When hospitalised in the state-run clinic,
I'm not the favourite patient like you are.
Marginalised, discriminated,
Just like an outsider.

When I choose religion,
I'm not faithful like you are.
Restricted worship in a demolished mosque,
Just inhuman.

When I'm in the orchestrated riot,
I'm not a survivor like you are.
No assurances of safety,
Just like a rape victim.

When the New Year turns,
I'm not a civilian like you are.
Under decades-long operations,
Just like an inventory item.

Even when I live in the country where I was born,
I can't call it mine like you do.
Without identity,
Just like an immigrant.

Even when I breathe the sky's air,
I'm not human like you are.
Without a reliable undertaker,
Just like a loner.

Even when I watch the sunrise,
I'm not living like you are.
Without the fertility of hope I live,
Just like a sandcastle.

Despite living on the apex of inhumanity
And the direness of immorality,
I'm quite surrounded.
My skin trembles
Just to feel once the full meaning of freedom,
My heart wishes
Just to walk once in my own world.

Nowadays, no one is like me.
Only myself.
Just a Rohingya!

ANONYMOUS

LOVESONG

MoliMeyer Bor Dala

En route to her house – they, three or four, travelled & feared
what the tiger will do – after it has consumed.

I have no fear of this tiger – in my dreams,
as I sleep, I hear her like a witch
doctor. She remains unafraid, chews
Paan constantly.

I discover Hajera's fragrance on the bird's handkerchief.

Near the King's palace, the rich build houses
of tin. They weigh grain to be sold
at the marketplace. On Saturdays, the teacher
who enlightens, who pities the masses – asks
Hajera to bring her a jug of water.

Asks after
Hajera had flung aside
                      her blanket of flowers.

You catch yourself slipping and falling
on the narrow road,
a black water jug – cracked on a dark night.

                                    Translated by Shehzar Doja
                                    Transcribed by Bilkis Akther
                                          Sung by Jani Alam

RO MEHROOZ

THE CUT BUD

Grandma planted
A seed. A few days later
It turned into twin plants.

They grew together
Like old friends.
Green leaves
Like butterfly wings.

   *

My drunk uncle came,
Cut one bud

              (Breath in silence)

   *

The other lives –
a bud bearing white flowers
Beside the cut bud.

              Ahhhhhhhh!

No scope for friendship.

THIDA SHANIA

FIRST DAY AT SCHOOL

In the morning
I was so excited,
I went to school early to find a seat
At the front of the class.

This chair is not for a kalar
Samaya told me.
And she sent me to the back
As I shredded.

That day, the lesson was
Discrimination (not curriculum),
The illnesses of the heart.

I went to school smiling,
Came back crying.

YAR TIN

ABOUT THOSE BORN INTO THIS PLACE

Though the land is fertile and the soil rich,
Born under an oppressive climate,
My body didn't grow like I'd hoped.
The blood-scented oxygen inhaled
Made my skin limp and lifeless;
Only sadness could take root in me.
Some find happiness only in oppression,
Others drift in the *samsara* of oppression;
To talk of people
All living under the same sky
Is to kill time;
Only the sound of hearts cracking
Under a depraved mind's bullying,
Bitter whispers
And uncertain sobs
Keep rubbing against my ears.

Though the land is fertile and the soil rich,
Because of the harsh, torturous seasons,
We who don't own mountains, the ocean,
The earth, the wide plains,
Don't own anything.

My lush green motherland,
Scorched by fire,
My once-pleasant kingdom,
Too wilted to show its face.
On the road paved for wandering,
Mine has strict limits;
The gates of the mosques that embodied peace
Are dressed in giant locks.
On the uneven scale of justice
We are assigned the lower end.

Though the land is fertile and the soil rich,
Because a divisive storm rages on,
Without contest,
The discriminated minutes
Turn my life into years,
And I who do not want to enter the ring
Get shoved into a fight,
I don't stand a chance, not even for a draw;
Under the lawless winner's mocking laughter
I steel myself
To keep hope from shattering,
And, sometimes, my tears draw blood.

Though the land is fertile and the soil rich,
This wild, restrictive wind
Keeps my education from ripening,
My hope from blooming;
My dignity has no chance to thrive,
There are no rights on my side.
Inside the prejudice of oppression,
My heart's tenderness is scarred.
When my spirit's wounds
Ache and shiver,
Why is there no bosom
For me to rest in, just for a moment?
Why must the balm of solution
Be so rare in this place?

Though the land is fertile and the soil rich,
In a quickening, genocidal gust,
Lives become fuel for weapons,
Consumed by flames;
Flesh becomes food for sea creatures,
And drops of blood, the price of dignity.
A whole lifetime turns to ash in the blink of an eye;
For an oppressor's fleeting pleasure,
Our lifespans are cruelly cut short,
Our hopes burned down;
The tears I shed for injustice,
The bitterness that I can only begin to tell but cannot end,

They keep adding to my heart's pages;
This genocidal history grows too thick, too heavy
For me to keep carrying around.

My Rohingya people and I,
With scarred hearts,
We walk across a thorn-strewn, death-riddled path,
Just to exist as respectable, proper humans;
We trudge on within the limits of truth;
Reach out to us with your human touch,
Give us permission to hope.

    Translated from the Burmese by Kenneth Wong & James Byrne

PHOTO: FOJIT SHEIKH BABU

PACIFIST FAROOQ

MY LIFE

Here's my life in brief...

I was a frog in a well,
A prisoner in the jail of fresh air.
In the dark, dark cosmos,
No days, just nights, nights.

A small cormorant survives
the genocidal waves
by being flung, crashing
into the world's strangeness.

Storm of racism, of hate –
This is my life.

Just like an action movie
In which you are the gangster.
Just like an actor who cannot discover his lines.

In Arakan, they kill and bury you
under the treasure of human rights.

ZAKI OVAIS

SOMEONE I'M AFRAID OF

I'm a hungry star in the sky,
covered by jealous clouds.

I'm a goldfish plant in the garden,
shaded from daylight.

I'm a fly in the kitchen, buzzing
on the boundary of a blind wall.

I'm a chicken under mother's wing,
confined to the narrows of a wattle.

I'm a dove on the street of Yangon,
jailed in the cage of inhumanity.

I'm the water flowing in Mayu river,
missing my partner – Air.

I'm a human in the universe,
denied the most basic rights.

I'm someone I'm afraid of.

MAUNG HLA SHWE

AN ORPHAN

He
> *(who always seeks parental love)*

He calls
> (all women – 'Mother')

But none is like
one's own
He – *(who understands the value)*
> of a mother's love.

*

A father *(would)*
> play.

A mother *(would)*
> care

day and night.

*

My heart extinguishes
> when I see *them*.

Who is there to play?
> *(with me…)*.

*

My life always lacked
> love and care

He – *(who thinks always)*
> his life as useless.

*

Why do I remain in this world ?	Who could love *me* – like my mother?

MAROON MOON

DAD

I colour in another page and stay calm –

    Dad, why won't you come back?

I look at all the empty cartoons I had coloured in earlier–

    Dad, why won't you talk to me?

Quietly, I pick up the colouring pencil of your favourite colour,
(Royal Blue) and scratch your name,
Beside my favourite cartoon character
(the Barbie doll you refused to buy) –

    Dad, why can't you hug me?

No more tears,
I turn each page backwards,
The first page has my name next to yours –
Dad, weren't we happy together?

I'm in grade 6 now,
A big girl, you wouldn't know me –

    Dad, why wouldn't you want to know?

RO PACIFIST

GIVE ME A CHANCE TO RESTART THIS LIFE

The quiet world of the womb,
where the uterus lines like a guard.

Mum was the president
of my safety –
blessings of the Almighty,
nine months
without cruelty.

Then, fortunate enough
(blessing my parents who had blessed me),
I journeyed into another world:
a hell, blooded
with terror sounds,
                explosions –
ash of villages burnt down.
over decades.

      My oxygen,
           not fresh like yours;
      arriving from years of bloodshed.

      My sky,
      not blue like yours;
      greyness of the smoky mountain.

It's a blessing on me
to live in the world
           safe and secure,
not full of vulnerabilities or brutality.

My childhood passed over youth,
   multiple scarring of the body,
      traumas in the sightstorm
          of my brain. A heavy lake
             tears in my eyes.

Hardly alive at all,
I wait here for your kindness.

Have mercy on me.
Give me the chance to restart this life,
to feel this world
like the womb of my mother.

PHOTO: SYED WASAMA DOJA

ANONYMOUS

LAMENT (A FISHERMAN'S SONG)

In just an empty boat
A fisherman has stolen my soul

That fisherman, he lures me   *– laughing, laughing*
He draws me in with his eyes

When the fisherman sailed off
with me – the groom
my housewife wandered the roadside alone
forever crying

My soul – it cries
as he lures me   *– laughing, laughing*
with his eyes.

The other fishermen
        they return from sea
and with some money
        they go to the market
to buy a red sari
        for my wife, (never to be)

Yet – my housewife's heart
still yearns for me.

The fisherman,
he looks at me   *– laughing, laughing*
and lures me
with his eyes.

Memories and talk of a wedding
now ten years past
cannot salve this terrible luck,
the misfortune of the Rohingya
never truly ends.

The fisherman, he calls
me again   *– laughing, laughing*
with his eyes

In just an empty boat
the fisherman had stolen my soul.

Transcribed by Bilkis Akther
Translated by Shehzar Doja
Sung by Jani Alam

RO ANAMUL HASAN

BEING ROHINGYA

    1

Tell me why my world is so different from others?
I grew up in a dark circle.

Where should I look for happiness?
Even time has no trace.

Why does the dream melt inside my eyes?
Reality is unauthorised.

My life has no luck. Why are lines of fate
Erased from my hand?

We all wear human organs. Am I not the same as you?
The world treats me like some other creature.

Numerous complaints on my lips,
But nobody tunes their ears to listen.

I sent a message once, it reached the sky,
Collided there, echoing, unanswered.

    2

I am baited for the hook
By those I trusted the most.
Let the sharks swallow me.

I am a target for the rifle-shoot
By those I honoured the most.
Let the shooters kill me.

I am slaughtered in cold blood
By those I obeyed the most.
Let the earth devour me.

I am handed a life sentence
By those I served the most.
Let the cell encircle me.

I am burnt alive in the bonfire
By those I relied on the most.
Let the fire incinerate me.

3

Are all these things about race or religion?

Am I not a human being?

I've been tolerating all this,

Just for being a Rohingya.

I was born in hell.

I was born in the bloodstream.

I was born on the battleground.

I saw on television they had rescued a man.

Many navy boats, helicopters.

But not one wooden boat was sent to rescue

Thousands of us drowning in the river.

RO MEHROOZ

BLOT OUT

I agree
The footprint has been blotted out from the path

But is the wire between two homes detached?
It has become an ocean between two homes

And who barred the coming breeze
From this ocean?

RO B. M. HAIRU

BEHIND LIFE

When I was in Myanmar,
I couldn't travel from one place to another –

    movement restriction for us.

When I was in Myanmar,
I couldn't worship inside the mosque –

    curfew order for us.

When I was in Myanmar,
I couldn't study freely in a Burmese school –

    discrimination for us.

When I was in Myanmar,
I couldn't play on my own land –

    soldiers marching on us.

When I was in Myanmar,
I couldn't sleep at night –

    relentless firing on us.

When I was in Myanmar,
I couldn't sell anything in the market –

    endless looting of us.

When I was in Myanmar,
I couldn't sow my own farm –

The 'us' of our land grabbed for Natala.

MAYYU ALI

THEY'RE KIND KILLERS

A stream of blood gushes
From where my husband and son were killed.
I watched
My baby snatched from me,
Thrown into the bonfire
Reflected in my eyes.

He couldn't even cry full song,
Burnt to fuel in a minute.
At least I didn't have to see the corpses like others did,
Nor did I have to bury them.
They're kind killers.

Killers who enjoy the hunt.
One asked for money and gold,
I gave him everything I owned, including my earrings
And then they raped me one after another.
The last one said:
I am not going to use my penis on you.
Instead, he used his knife.
They set me alight and left me for dead.
I find myself silent and bleeding.
The world is too brave to watch us being killed.

THIDA SHANIA

SAVE ME

Snipers shoot father and mother,
drag their little son along the street

    Save me

Dictators blast atom bombs,
only mother is left

    Save me

Soldiers burn houses and villages,
kill men and their sons,
molest and rape the girl

    Save me

Scream to save lives.
Scream to save dignity.
Scream to save humanity.

Keep screaming, until your scream
pierces the office block.

No matter who he or she is,
young, old,
Palestinian, Yemeni,
Syrian, Kashmiri,
or even a Rohingya

    Save me

    Save me

    Save me

MAUNG HLA SHWE

MY ARAKAN

Arakan, my birthplace
                fallen.

What do you feel
   when you see your birthplace
      bald-headed?
               My Arakan torn
               to pieces.

The men and the boys are slaughtered.

What do you feel
   when you see your loved ones
      in blood river?

               My Arakan torn
               to pieces.

The women and the girls are raped.

What do you feel
   when you see
      your sister raped?

               My Arakan torn
               to pieces.

Thousands of homes burnt
                      down.

What do you feel
   when you see
      your home burnt down?

        My Arakan torn
        to pieces.

Walking among the mass graves.

What do you feel
    when you see your sibling's corpse
        inside a mass grave?

        My Arakan torn
        to pieces.

Millions of Rohingya forced to be refugees.

What do you feel
    when the days pass
        in homelessness?

        My beautiful Arakan
        torn to pieces.

AZAD MOHAMMED

MISFORTUNE

Around the world
people use materials
    in defence –

        umbrellas for rain.
            Jackets for cold.
                Sunglasses for heat.

                    Umbrellas.
                    Umbrellas.

In Cox's Bazaar, no trees, no home, no stream –
not like our golden Arakan.

In our golden land, the trees give shade.
In Cox's Bazaar, tarpaulin offers heat.

    You can't control tears with sweat.

Oh, weather, my question to you,
as one of many genocide survivors, is why –

why in this treeless, shadeless refugee camp,
    why, like the Myanmar government,
        do you still set us on fire?

YASMIN ULLAH

BIRTH

I was born
under the blazing sun of a hot summer,
I was born from a massacre survivor.
Woman, sister, wife, mother –
my grandmother,
the last girl from her entire family tree,
left with only a nine year-old brother
at thirteen
from her little village back in 1942,
back when the world strived to resolve
problems with wars,
not peace.

I was born among a million displaced and stateless people
who go out to the field,
farming, fishing until their backs
break. Labour of jobs, barely paid,
the pennies we made
snatched.
We weren't looking for riches,
nor to exert their power over anyone –
my people work hard,
only to survive.

I was born under a sun that burns through skin.
Rohingya are dark.
If they say we look like beggars,
we really become beggars –
no free will,
no choices left.

I was born to a country that rejected us,
even our own people disowned us.
Dictatorship leaves a bitter taste
of poverty in the mouth,

they push us to the lowest of the low.
We self-identify as 'Rohingya'
so we won't lose the last glimpse of
history and its triumphs.
How great we once were.
How we have been trampled into
extermination –

I see you shake your head,
asking, 'how?
when the light of democracy shines so bright?'
I want to believe it,
but truth is more often than not
unfortunate –
Burma is cruel and genocidal,
yet it is my homeland.

I was born among rows of dead infants
burned alive, thrown into fire,
drowned in water,
fallen into the river,
to escape the punishment
of crimes they didn't commit.

I was born from malnourished children,
the skin and bones of elders,
impoverished, stricken, shoeless.
Since when did shoes become a luxury?

Blood swims through my veins,
the agony of women
shapes me into a living body –
women who, in every attack,
every massacre,
were raped, their souls assaulted –
women who find themselves victims
of human trafficking,
sex trafficking,
because that for them is
better,

compared to living in this
soul-shattering,
hellish reality.

Every rape,
every assault
leaves women more
bare,
more raw,
more exposed,
more vulnerable.

I was born of loving mothers
who, despite their plight,
give and give everything for their children,
no questions asked,
so they could have the future
their mothers were denied.
Even if it means carrying the children in their two tired arms,
bleeding internally, excessively from
their gang rapes,
their tortures,
their throats slit,
their flesh sliced,
hours before fleeing.

Rohingya mothers run with all their might,
hoping to make it across
to the other side,
feet worn by thorns and pebbles,
mothers who bled and cried but kept going –
little did they know
they would be torn apart from their children,
the very moment makeshift rafts
capsized.
Their will to live was strong,
but the river's current
separates humanity,
is stronger.

I was born of innocent fathers
who kept running from
their death sentence –
it's like a game, if you lose,
you stop breathing.
Rohingya fathers dragged out
of homes, kidnapped, beaten,
jailed without trial.
And if there's a chance,
if they survive, and walk out of prison,
free,
they are still imprisoned
by the vicious cycle of being
Rohingya.
They say our sin can only be atoned
by suffering and death.

I was born of the people whose long exiles
are destined –
our long journey of pain
the world took over half century to take notice.
I lost count how many times
we became refugees,
I lost count how many left their cities
never allowed back –
leaving children behind,
turning their backs on family,
outside the comfort of *home*,
alone and struggling.
Our feet are so tired,
broken heels bleed,
the mud we walked through
dried, hardened.
If we walk the entire earth
barefoot,
would we ever find
a home?

I was born of children whose eyes
speak the story of tragedy,

eyes that saw parents slain,
bullets dodged, landmines –
children hear more gunshots and death messages
than their own mothers' soothing voice.
Children dreaming nightmares
over reality –
flames rise to the sky,
a tall tower,
taking everything they ever loved.
Every night, chilled screams
from mothers, sisters,
lifeless bodies of fathers, brothers.

I was born of deep scars,
from decades of beating
and the deliberate process of annihilation,
trying not give into those traffickers.
We became *boat people*,
landless, no country would accept us –
instead, living in the ocean's vast uncertainty
that could swallow us whole.
How is it better to live in old boats, small rafts,
on the verge of breaking, how?

I was born of tears that continue to flow,
from the direction of hope to hopelessness.

I was born of wounds that still burn,
that still bleed,
until tomorrow,
when more wounds will be inflicted,
when our entire bodies will be
forced into hand-dug, shallow graves.

I was born under unjust
ruling greed and power.
I was born of loud cries,
of homes being torn,
burned, bulldozed –
born of the people whose innocence

is not good enough to vindicate them
from the agonies of the future.

I was born of tired backs, exhausted bodies,
looking for provisions
so hard to come by,
walking miles carrying water
to makeshift huts,
without help –
water or mud,
you have to drink to survive.

I was born of empty stomachs,
tongues dried and parched lips,
from starvation of food and water
for months on end.

I was born of the forced crooked smile
blurred with tears,
the slow fade of resilience.

I was born as one of the forgotten,
of those the world doesn't quite remember.
But at least I was born,
so you can hear me speaking up,
so you, the world, can listen.

This could take generations to mend,
our losses are irreplaceable.
We taste fear in every breath.
It's not enough to hope for
the generosity of helping hands
or consoling voices,
I want the ears of love,
the heart of justice
that believes
that as much we are victims
there is potential in our social contribution.
There is more to being Rohingya than exodus.

So, please,
look at me,
my people, us,
through the lens
you reserve for someone
special,
wholesome, human –
not so different
from you.

The complex case of the Rohingya
might easily be solved
if we all just brush up on our
empathy.

PHOTO: FOJIT SHEIKH BABU

MAUNG ABDUL KHAN

NEW HOPE

This journey – *anguished*
I am – at the last – *stage*
Facing | *failure*

He – is – the – future – me
She – is – the – future – me
Yes – they – are | *My*
Son and daughter
my
future

PHOTO: FOJIT SHEIKH BABU

MAROON MOON

OUR FAIRYTALE

Why does it hurt this much?
Why do I love you and miss you so much?
Why are you the weight of the whole world?

Touch and sight, in absence,
Your shadow lives. You are everything.

Where have you been?

Lingering trail of your scent.
      Once a stranger – mysterious, unknown.
           Everything unknown that I want
To know.
I admire you in secret.

Was our meeting one of the prophecies foretold?

At times, your presence makes no sense.
I can't really tell when I fell for you,
My soul giggles,
You can hear me humming joy, only…

The fear of being
      adrift leaves me helplessly
            sobbing,

When love is this pure it holds onto hope.

ZAKI OVAIS

WATER

Somewhere plenty,
Somewhere enough,
Somewhere in tube-wells,
Somewhere in natural lakes,
Somewhere man-made in a factory,
Pumped, filtered, packed.

Sometimes frozen,
Sometimes warmed up,
Sometimes boiled,
Could it be timeless?

      Water, water – it is.

Some waste it,
Some can afford to buy it,
Some live a million miles away from it.

      Water, water – it is.

Black, white, red,
Cattle, fly, man,
Plant, shrub, tree,
All living things exist,
Can't survive without it.

      Water, water – it is.

Sometimes transport,
Sometimes taking us away in the floods,
Sometimes rainwater filling our thirst,
Sometimes jailing us in the downpour.

      Water, water – it is.

RO B. M. HAIRU

TELL ME WHAT WE ARE GUILTY OF!

The Arakan turned into a battlefield,
non-stop gunfire and torture.
Widow meets widower,
The world outside too weak to save us.
Tell me what we are guilty of!

The Arakan turned into a central jail,
non-stop arrests and detention.
Some were killed in hiding.
The world outside was too blind to see us.
Tell me what we are guilty of!

The Arakan turned into genocide.
Non-stop raping and murdering.
Some were thrown screaming into the fire.
The world outside was too quiet to hear.
Tell me what we are guilty of!

Disaster's misery breathed on us.
Where is the humanity? Where is the equality?
Was it just for being Rohingya or Muslim?
The world outside must be pitiless.
Tell me what we are guilty of!

YAR TIN

TOO MUCH BITTERNESS

To make rhymes out of gunshots,
To make poetry out of death and destruction,
This heart of mine is not skilled enough.

Bullets and hatred
Rule our surroundings;
Greedy to save a life,
The Rohingyas of this land, this country,
Fled where they could in chaos;
Hundreds of legs on the run
Crushed and broken along the way;
For some, it's a victory parade;
For others, it's apocalypse.

We are
Like birds in a blue sky backdrop
With no chance to take flight;
The smoke rising from our nest
Takes the place of clouds.

Might as well let it rain –
To quench the fire
Devouring our homes,
To soothe the innocent children tossed into flames,
The old and the weak trapped inside.
As if raindrops could extinguish them all.

The tears of those who have lost everything,
If only they hadn't been wrongly displaced,
Might have been enough to put out
Our fire-ravaged nests;
Might have offered shelter
To the little birds tossed into the fire,
The old and the weak trapped inside.

For the human rights we haven't tasted
Since we were born from the womb,
For the right to live as humans, among humans,
What else must we give up?

When our sacrifice
To secure a little piece of dignity
Became disproportionate,
In return,
We were honoured with
The title of
The world's most oppressed people.

For wanting to shed this title,
We who call Arakan home
Are labelled, *those who enter illegally,*
Terrorists,
And discriminated.

All is well,
At the limit of my eye is the sky,
I shall stretch out my hope all the way;
Along a path paved with lives,
I will forge ahead.

But
When I have to use another's tragedy
As pages for my poetry,
My heart shudders and aches.

Translated from the Burmese by Kenneth Wong

AHTARAM SHINE

MEMORY OF TORTURE

When I was in Myanmar,
I was tortured beyond sin.

Inhumanity of the Burmese military,
desire in their laws.

Before the British colonists,
to be Burmese meant to be multi-ethnic.
We lived together peacefully

    (969 monks broke the silence).

Once upon a time,
my country was a green forest

    (969 monks burned it down).

When I sleep at night,
a horrible nightmare appears,
I wake up, my heart exhausted.

When somebody tells me about anything bad,
I think of Myanmar military brutality.

I'm trying to free myself
from the memory of torture.

I want to erase my mind.

MAROON MOON

HOW?

How do you turn your back on tears?
How do you hush a weeping sigh?
How do you abandon a part of yourself?
How do you look away from the innocent?
How do you deny the warmth of your breast?
How do you let innocence drown in the vastness of self-doubt?
How do you call questions mind games?
How do you withdraw assurance's mercy?
How do you confine someone to lurking darkness?
How do you convince them every mistake is a step closer to failure?

Someone tripped and kept falling.
What else can I say?
The living transformed into the living dead.

MAYYU ALI

A ROHINGYA REFUGEE

I can be killed here in Bangladesh.
My body can earn a proper funeral.
Going back to Myanmar would be foolish,
Not even the assurance of a funeral!

Triggering suicidal ideas in Cox's Bazaar
While my sisters are trafficked and my brothers kidnapped.
Every refugee wishes to go back home,
Why do I need to deny myself?

Despite the longest running mind movie,
I still shout for justice.
All I want is to live again in my own home,
A safe life, to enjoy my rights.

The world I knew has gone,
My people were killed and displaced.
It's the fourth time I have fled Bangladesh,
My life is spent just trying to survive.

I always ask myself during repatriation:
Is this the last time?
Could I be fortunate enough to escape again?
This time it is different. My heart is asking me.

PACIFIST FAROOQ

THE HEART'S BURNING SMELL

I once seeded a plant of love inside me.
I lived in its shadow and ate the fruits. The plant
survived for a few weeks but soon died.
The sun in this world lacks light.

In those weeks when it was alive,
The plant of love grew into a tree.
My conscience ingested the toxin,
I consumed my brain to protect my body.

Back then, I was a boy playing with fire,
I wanted to open the plain of happiness.
Fire torched the heart of the plant. And now,
The burning smell just keeps on spreading.

PHOTO: FOJIT SHEIKH BABU

RO MEHROOZ

BROKEN MIRROR

I wake up to the speaking mirror.

To the tragedy, the scare
of the hitting bullet.

*

I cannot dare to look
at the mirror, looking
at the mirror looking back.

*

The bullet flew towards my head.
I ducked down and ran.

The bullet smashes the mirror,
shards scatter over the floor.

        (Breathe –)

*

Today, I see the mirror
In the taxi window,
In the barbers shop.

MAUNG ABDUL KHAN

SURVIVOR

In the battlefield
I am a survivor.

On the sand
I am a traveller
alone,
surviving
painful heat.

On the *sampan*,
in the risky waves,
I am a traveller
surviving

under the rain,
I am a traveller
umbrella-less,
surviving.

In the noise,
I am a traveller
feeling
alone
in the crowd,

searching
the deep breath
of
peace.

YASMIN ULLAH

THE UNFAMILIAR HOME

I keep missing a place I barely know.

Home – untouched
families I can never return to,
how I long
        for their
                hugs.

Countries are known
for architecture, buildings, landscapes,
so accessible on-screen,
but on-screen – how can you know
anything
  about beauty   missed.

None of it makes it
to the cover of magazines,
        yet I wish you knew this place,
my place, my home,
taken from me,

        I wish – you saw the family
they ripped a-
          part from me,

I wish you knew
    through even one or two
                   pictures,
so you would

                at least be able
                            to relate,
and maybe… only maybe,
you would cherish this place
                        as much – as I do,
perhaps you would
    try to protect it,
from the tyrannical oppression
                    of the innocents,
            in their own home.

How –
        I wish
                you could
                        know.

PHOTO: FOJIT SHEIKH BABU

ANONYMOUS

MOTHER ARAKAN

Fleeing the Golden Land
we have become (these)
nomads
on other shores –
peace does not come
                      for us

How is it, that somehow, we were able
                                    to leave
home? We could not linger any more

When Arakan floats up – remembering – these eyes
                                      are mournful.

Oh these! – assortments and abundance of fruits, such richness we have
discarded – on the path to these other shores
no one asks about us,
everywhere there is speech – but
no one speaks   (about us)
Oh mothers and sisters!

                Where can we go to achieve some peace?

Oh countrymen – (who calls like a flute)
            where can we go
                    in search of solace?

I wonder inside so many fragments
            my life(span)
                diminishes

When Arakan floats up – remembering – these eyes
are mournful.

Transcribed by Bilkis Akther
Translated by Shehzar Doja
Sung by Jani Alam

RO MEHROOZ

NIGHT-BLOOMING JASMINE

O moon uncle, moon uncle, please hear me.
Come to the wedding wearing white.
For you, the buds of the night-blooming jasmine wait.
The wind will blow, blow slowly, the buds will fall.
The whole fence will smell of its scent.

O moon uncle, moon uncle, please hear me.
Come to the wedding wearing white.
My elder sister said she will wear buds
Of the night-blooming jasmine,
Knitting its threads into a wreath.
She will dye henna on her hands with friends.
Her wedding is in two days, will you come?

O moon uncle, moon uncle, please hear me.
Come to the wedding wearing white.

Translated from Rohingya by James Byrne and the author

HASNA HENA

Ōo sānda mamu sānda mamu hotha funo sai
Fūd. Dhola rōng fidhi mūnthu ayyo sai
Tuallai sōi thakkye Hasna Hena'r holī
Boyar āibo irir irir, holī zāiboi zhori
UDhan-BhiDa aga-gura dibo khushboo gori…

Ōo sānd mamu sānd mamu hotha funo sai
Fūd hola rōng fidhi mūnthu ayyo sai
Bubu hoyye māthat dībo Hasna Hena'r holī
Futhat maze gāñthi gāñthi fulor sora bañdhī
Āro dībo hatōt mōodhi fuajja zerfuain mili
Dui din bāde bubu'r bīya, bīya.t āiba ni…

Ōo sānd mamu sānd mamu hotha funo sai
Fūd. Dhola rōng fidhi bīya.t ayyo sai…

NOTES

p. 26 – ANONYMOUS, 'Lovesong':
MoliMeyer means the daughter of Moli. *Bor Dala* refers to a ceremony where the groom's family delivers a basket of gifts for the bride. *Paan* is the leaves of the betel plant which is frequently wrapped around tobacco or fruit and chewed. It has a pleasant effect, and is like a drug.

p. 28 – THIDA SHANIA, 'First Day at School':
Kalar is a racial slur for Rohingya used by Burmese Buddhists, meaning 'foreigner'. A *Samaya* is school madam or teacher in Burmese.

p. 29 – YAR TIN, 'About Those Born into This Place':
Samsara, from Buddhism, refers to the cycle of birth, death and rebirth as being continuous, dependent on karma.

p. 32 –PACIFIST FAROOQ, 'My Life':
The 'You' in the poem refers to the Burmese government.

p. 43 – Ro B. M. HAIRU, 'Behind Life':
Natala refers to Buddhists brought from upper Myanmar to settle on Rohingya in Northern Rakhine State, Myanmar.

p. 44 – MAYYU ALI, 'They're Kind Killers':
This poem is based on an account from a rape survivor of the Tula Toli Massacre which was carried out by the Burmese military in Rankine State in 2017.

p. 48 – AZAD MOHAMMED, 'Misfortune':
The poem refers to a fire in the camps that happened on the second day of the workshops, on the 24 April, 2019, thereby preventing Azad Mohammed's participation. The poem also alludes to the threat of further fires occurring in such dry and hot conditions.

p. 62 – AHATRAM SHINE, 'Memory of Torture':
'969' is the name of the nationalist, militant wing of Buddhism in Myanmar (also known as Ma Ba Tha or the Organisation for the Protection of Race and Religion), which spreads anti-Rohingya propaganda widely throughout the country.

p. 67 – Maung Abdul Khan, 'Survivor':
A *sampan* is a small, U-shaped boat with a flat bottom, generally used for fishing or transportation in coastal areas or rivers. It is unusual for sampans to sail far from land, as they do not have the means to survive rough weather.

AFTERWORD: AN INTERVIEW WITH MAYYU ALI

Note: This interview was conducted over email in January 2019 and was originally published in World Literature Today *(April, 2019). What follows is an edited version of the original.*

JAMES BYRNE (JB): *Cox's Bazaar is the largest refugee camp in the world. The Tatmadaw (Burmese military) army is on one side, the Bangladeshi army is on the other. What is it like for the Rohingya to live in a place like this?*

MAYYU ALI (MA): The Naf river separates Myanmar and Bangladesh. The water of the Naf flows through creeks into Myanmar. As an exiled Rohingya from Myanmar in Bangladesh's refugee camp, I can still breathe the air of my motherland when it flies through the sky. And the green forest in Arakan that I see seems to want me to embrace it.

On the Myanmar side, the Burmese Tatmadaw are still committing human rights' abuses to Rohingyas living there. In Bangladesh, the Bangaladeshi army have been providing refuge for more than one million Rohingya who have escaped the killings in Myanmar. I am just one among many.

Surviving in a place like this is like living in two different worlds at the same time, one which revolves around the cruel inhumanity in Myanmar, the other around the safety of humanity in Bangladesh. Writing about being a Rohingya in such a situation is a battle between trying to survive and making the voices of people who are counted as forgotten in the world heard.

JB: *You write in English. How far is your decision to write poetry in English a response to colonial oppression and how difficult has it been for the Rohingya to create their own poetry in the Rohingya language?*

MA: Rohingyas were kings in Arakan. The Rohingya language was used in Arakan courts. Historical evidence, such as stone inscriptions and coins, shows that the Rohingya are a *bona fide* ethnic group which has been living for centuries in Arakan. and which belongs to a distinct culture, tongue and scripture.

During Rakhine dynasties, there were wars and aggression. Decades later, Myanmar was under colonial oppression for more than a hundred years. On 4 January 1948, Myanmar got its independence. Since 1960, the country has been administered by military juntas.

During colonialism, people lost touch with their own culture and tradition. And during administration under the military juntas, many people, especially the Rohingya, were targeted because of their national identity which, even though it had existed for so long, they then lost.

Thus, I was born to a Rohingya parent in Myanmar following decades of state-sponsored persecution. I learnt the Rohingya language without learning its written form which is two hundred years old and uses a version of Arabic script. Whilst learning the Rohingya language, I found that the culture and literature of my people had been eliminated through social targeting. The experiences in my life have taught me to write in English rather than in Burmese, because I want people from all over the world to understand why my people have been discriminated against for decades.

And yet Rohingya still belongs to the culture that my grandpa knew. He would often sing me to sleep with songs and poetry written in our dialect. Unfortunately, today, we have lost our language.

JB: *Recently you and I have been talking about ways of writing poems which document what you can see. How difficult is this, given your desire to share the Rohingya experience with the outside world? How might activism and imagism operate together in a poem for you?*

MA: As I grew older in Myanmar's west, I encountered a world where every human right was denied to us. I learnt how we (Rohingya) were marginalised and discriminated against religiously, socially and politically.

Despite this, I managed to receive an education at a government-run school in a rural area. In 2008, I passed my matriculation exams which I needed to enter university. In 2012, anti-Muslim riots spread across Rakhine State. After this, hundreds of Rohingya students were banned from attending Sittway University. I finished my first and second years in 'English Specialization' at the University, but when the violence broke out in 2012, I was prevented from continuing my studies.

If you are a Rohingya in Rakhine State, access to reading good books or popular magazines is rare. Movement is severely restricted even from one township to another. At an early age, life taught me to undertake the writing of poems and articles that look back to the pain and despair of my people. Thus, writing became a passion in my blood.

Writing for Rohingya people is activism. For me, a Rohingya, and a victim of the slow-burning genocide in Myanmar, imagism is far removed from activism.

JB: Which poets did you have access to as a Rohingya poet when you were living in Myanmar? Did movements like Khitsan ('testing the times') and Khitpor ('modern poetry') matter to you, as they did to Burmese poets?

MA: No Rohingya is officially considered a writer or poet. So, as somebody who is marginalised, you do not have easy access to sources of inspiration. I just know those poets I read as part of the school curriculum, like Shakespeare, Longfellow, Cristina Rossetti etc, but I didn't have real access to any poets.

In 2008, when I passed the matriculation, I came across *Best English* and *Light of English* magazines in Myanmar. I sent them poems and, over time, sixteen were published. These magazines were published every month. When the anti-Muslim riots broke out in 2012 in Rakhine State, having access to, or buying, magazines from downtown, or posting submissions to them at post office, was restricted. Now I have lost touch with the magazines that I enjoyed so much.

For me, the Khitsan and Khitpor movements both existed at the same time that I, a Rohingya poet, was being brought up at the heart of Myanmar's genocide.

JB: You had witnessed many traumatic experiences in Rakhine before travelling to Bangladesh. In the last few years, you've developed into one of the leading new Rohingya humanitarian workers, someone who recently set up the Rohingya Youth Empowerment Centre in the camps, educating the Rohingya from within, resisting the often vested interests of NGOs. How were your experiences in Myanmar important to the humanitarian aid work you are doing now? And can you tell us a little more about the YEC?

MA: For decades, Rohingya people have had severely restricted access to healthcare, education, freedom of movement, social activities, etc. The Rohingya are Myanmar's most vulnerable community and Western Rakhine State, the country's second poorest state, is where Rohingya people have been living for generations. It is one of the world's most isolated zones for humanitarian aid. Myanmar is responsible for the persecution, subjection and vulnerability of my community. Despite being the perpetrator of these crimes, the Myanmar government often stops the flow of humanitarian aid and restricts INGOs and Agencies from carrying out their activities in Rakhine. Northern Rakhine State's maternal mortality rate is double that of Myanmar's national average, which, at 200 deaths per 100,000 live births, is already one of Asia's worst. In Buthidaung and Maungdaw, malnutrition rates rival those of war-torn regions in sub-Saharan Africa.

When I was stopped from attending Sittway University in 2012, I joined Action Contre la Faim (ACF), a French-based INGO tackling malnutrition in Rakhine State. I was working for ACF at the time my village was burnt down and we were forced to flee to Bangladesh during the killings on 25 August, 2017.

I continue to understand, as I did then, how crucial humanitarian work is for Rohingya communities to be able to survive. As you mention, last year in Balukhali camp at Cox's Bazaar, I founded the Youth Empowerment Centre (YEC). We conduct workshops that focus on rebuilding lives and providing training for Rohingya youth, especially in peace-building, leadership, management, creative thinking, etc. We believe that an empowered youth will be the bed-rock on which the community can be rebuilt. We hope Rohingya will be a civilised community very soon.

JB: How can the Rohingya people use their voice to mobilize whilst living in the camps? With daily survival the main priority and a language, as well as a people, that have been suppressed, are artists able to make responses to the experiences they are living through? If not, what could change to make this happen?

MA: Here in the camps, everyone struggles to survive each day. We need everything here. For Rohingyas who have been seeking peace and justice, daily life teaches them what the greatest concerns are – formal education for their children, birth certificates for newborn babies, freedom of movement, proper access to healthcare, enough food, safe shelter, etc. There are Rohingya parents who want formal education for their children.

There are Rohingya youths who want to rebuild community life. There are students who want to continue their studies.

On social media such as Facebook, there are young Rohingya people who have been trying hard, writing poetry and articles. There are Rohingya bloggers and young poets who write poems and articles in Burmese and English, people like me. They want to be a voice for their people. We want to change lives. We have the same dreams as others in the world.

JB: In the first poem I ever read of yours, 'That's Me, A Rohingya', I remember the stanza: 'Even when I watch the sunrise, / I'm not living like you are. / Without the fertility of hope I live, / Just like a sandcastle.' It quickly struck me that, far from being 'hopeless', your poems read like powerfully active survival mantras. But how, for the Rohingya, can hope genuinely find a way?

MA: We had hopes that Aung San Suu Kyi would help us. She was our hero when we lived in Myanmar. After she came to power with a landslide victory in the 2015 election, she turned a blind eye and now does not care about the situation for the Rohingya in Myanmar. The world's fastest exodus of Rohingya people happened under her administration in August 2017. She is a leader, and therefore is morally responsible for her country's minority people, the Rohingya. But she has failed, and the Rohingya have lost their last hope.

On the other hand, the international community has not yet done enough, and so justice for the Rohingya, most of whom are living in the camps, or in a wider diaspora in neighbouring countries, remains elusive.

If we don't have support from inside Myanmar or from the international community, we will have to find hope within ourselves. One of the most important changes that would enable the Rohingya to rebuild their lives would be to allow them to make the most of where they live with what they have. To make this happen, those Rohingya leaders living overseas will have to take more responsibility and prioritise rebuilding activities. Every Rohingya should contribute to rebuilding a civilised community.

When, as a Rohingya, I'm referred to as one of the world's most persecuted people, I'm determined, with a passion that flows through all my veins, to become one of the world's most hard-working people.

JB: The false promise of repatriation in October was resisted by the Rohingya at the end of last year. For you, what is the best way out of the camps? Where do you want to be?

MA: I want to go back home. Myanmar is my motherland – we've been living there for generations. We fought for independence and paid with the same blood and sweat as other ethnic groups in the country. We love our motherland like others do. Historically, geographically, ancestrally, we belong there.

In a single decade, we have fled and returned many times. Every Rohingya wishes to go back to their homeland in a safe, dignified and voluntary way. We want peace and justice first. Perpetrators of the violence should be held to account. The Myanmar government should ensure safe repatriation and proper rehabilitation for us. They should restore citizenship rights to the Rohingya. The international community should stand firm until the Rohingya people enjoy the same rights as other ethnic groups in Myanmar.

CONTRIBUTORS

(Note: many of the Rohingya poets mentioned below use a pen-name. This is mostly for aesthetic reasons, but it also helps to protect their real identity. In some cases, only basic information is given to protect poets' safety).

BILKIS AKHTER works for the Friendship NGO in Bangladesh as a schoolteacher. She is currently working in the Rohingya camps.

JANI ALAM is a Rohingya folk singer who keeps the songs and oral traditions of his mother tongue alive by performing them to audiences in the refugee camps. He is currently living in Cox's Bazaar after being forced out from Myanmar.

MAYYU ALI is a young Rohingya poet, writer and humanitarian activist who runs the Youth Empowerment Centre in the refugee camp at Cox's Bazaar. His poems have appeared in *Modern Poetry in Translation, rohingyablogger.com, World Literature Today*, as well as *Best English* and *Light of English* magazines in Myanmar. His articles have featured in *Al Jazeera, Dhaka Tribune*, on CNN and in the *Financial Times*. Recently he published *The Blossom*, including some of his earliest poems, which was distributed around the camps.

FOJIT SHEIKH BABU is a staff photo journalist for the daily newspaper *Alokito Bangladesh* and lives in Dhaka. In 2018, his exhibition 'Who are the new 'Boat People'?' was part of Edge Hill University's Festival of Ideas.

JAMES BYRNE is renowned for his commitment to international poetries and translation. He co-edited *Bones Will Crow: 15 Contemporary Burmese Poets* (Arc Publications, 2012). He is the International Editor for Arc and author of five books of poems, including *White Coins* and *The Caprices* (both by Arc, 2015 & 2019). Byrne is Senior Lecturer in poetry and poetics at Edge Hill University. A translated book of his *Selected Poems / Poemas Selectos* is published by Buenos Aires Poetry.

SHEHZAR DOJA is a poet and Founder / Editor-in-Chief of the literary journal, *The Luxembourg Review*. His work has appeared in publications such as *New Welsh Review, Pratik, Voice and Verses, Fresh from the Fountain* and *Fundstücke-Trouvailles*. He was on the Jury Panel for the Literary Prize at the Printemps des Poètes festival in Luxembourg, 2018 and again in 2019. His poetry collection *Drift* was published by UPL / Monsoon Letters.

PACIFIST FAROOQ is a poet, educator, writer, teacher, translator, human rights activist, peace builder, footballer, former singer and songwriter. He was born in 2000 in Buthidaung, Northern Rakhine State, Myanmar. He completed his matriculation examination with two distinctions in 2016 but, like many Rohingya, was prevented from pursuing further education. In August 2018, he narrowly escaped from the genocidal operations of the Tatmadaw and now lives as a refugee in Cox's Bazaar refugee camp.

Ro B. M. HAIRU is a Rohingya student, born in 1998. He passed his matriculation exam in 2015. Ro wishes to become a famous poet from the Rohingya community and has written several poems and stories.

Ro ANAMUL HASAN was born in 1997. He is from a poor family near Maungdaw township, Arakan. He passed his matriculation exam in 2014 and lives in the refugee camps in Cox's Bazaar, having previously known relatives killed, arrested and tortured by the Burmese military.

MAUNG ABDUL KHAN is a Rohingya Youth activist, writer and poet who runs an online education channel for the Rohingya, called the Rohingya Learning Centre, which can be found on Facebook and YouTube. His poems and philosophical thoughts (quotes) have appeared in monthly Myanmar magazines such as *Best English*, *Light of English* and *Youth Magazine* from 2006 to 2012. He was a Rohingya Youth Leader for the youth club programme of BOSCO/UNHCR from 2014 to 2018. Maung graduated from Sittway University with a degree in Statistics in 2009. He had to flee his country in 2012.

Ro MEHROOZ is a young Rohingya poet, lyricist, computer programmer and activist who has written poems mostly in Rohingya and English, but also a few in Burmese and Urdu. He trains young Rohingya students in computer programming in the refugee camp at Cox's Bazaar and believes in reading poetry as a way of travelling through the minds of others in the world.

AZAD MOHAMMED is from Myanmar and now lives in Cox's Bazaar refugee camp. In his free time he writes poems that relate to Rohingya community living. His dream is to become a professional photographer.

MAROON MOON is the pen name of Dr. Yasmin Haroon, a poet and Rohingya blogger brought up in the Middle East.

ZAKI OVAIS is a new Rohingya poet. He wrote some of his first poems during the workshops (including 'I'm someone I'm afraid of'). Zaki is also a community development worker who fled Myanmar.

RO PACIFIST is a Rohingya refugee currently surviving in a makeshift settlement in Cox's Bazaar. He has, since the age of thirteen, been interested in writing poems, stories and articles. He teaches English to Rohingya students in the camps.

THIDA SHANIA is a young Rohingya poet who has published her poems on *The Art Garden*, a Rohingya poetry website.

AHTARAM SHINE is 23 years old, one of ten siblings. He is originally from Myanmar (Southern Maungdaw Odaung), but currently resides in Cox's Bazaar refugee camp. He completed his high school education from Maungdaw, Muma Kayandan in 2014.

MAUNG HLA SHWE is 19 years old. His home village is Sabby Gone, in Maung Daw township, Arakan State. He currently lives in Balukhali, Cox's Bazaar, working as a teacher at the Community Rebuilding Centre-Education (CRC- E) in the camps.

YAR TIN is a Rohingya poet and short story writer from Rakhine State. He is a blogger. He writes poems and articles for *Rohingya Today* (formerly *Rohingya Blogger*).

YASMIN ULLAH is a Rohingya social justice activist born in Northern Rakhine State, Myanmar. She fled to Thailand in 1995 along with her parents and remained a stateless refugee until 2011. She now lives in Canada, and is President of the Rohingya Human Rights Network, a non-profit group led by activists across Canada in advocacy and raising public awareness of the Rohingya genocide. She is completing an undergraduate degree in political science. Yasmin is also actively involved in creating more accessible mosques and places of spirituality for those with special needs through her work in co-directing HAMDA (Helping All Muslims with Different Abilities).

KENNETH WONG is the author of *A Prayer for Burma* (Santa Monica Press, 2003). He is a Burmese-American author and translator, born and raised in Myanmar, now living in the USA. His short stories, essays, and poetry translations have appeared in *Granta* (Boston University), *Grain, San Francisco Chronicle, Myanmar Times, The Irrawaddy,* and *Eleven Eleve*n journal (California College of the Arts), among others. He teaches Beginning and Intermediate Burmese at the University of California, Berkeley.

CPSIA information can be obtained
at www.ICGtesting.com
Printed in the USA
LVHW090543120521
687090LV00007B/807